4. Peter's Denial

John 18: 14–27

Now Caiaphas was he, which gave counsel to the Jews, that it was expedient that one man should die for the people. And Simon Peter followed Jesus, and so did another disciple: that disciple was known unto the high priest, and went in with Jesus into the palace of the high priest. But Peter stood at the door without. Then went out that other disciple, which was known unto the high priest, and spake unto her that kept the door, and brought in Peter. Then saith the damsel that kept the door unto Peter, Art not thou also one of this man's disciples? He saith, I am not. And the servants and officers stood there, who had made a fire of coals; for it was cold: and they warmed themselves: and Peter stood with them, and warmed himself. The high priest then asked Jesus of his disciples, and of his doctrine. Jesus answered him, I spake openly to the world; I ever taught in the synagogue, and in the temple, whither the Jews always resort; and in secret have I said nothing. Why askest thou me? Ask them which heard me, what I have said unto them: behold, they know what I said. And when he had thus spoken, one of the officers which stood by struck Jesus with the palm of his hand, saying, Answerest thou the high priest so? Jesus answered him, If I have spoken evil, bear witness of the evil: but if well, why smitest thou me? Now Annas had sent him bound unto Caiaphas the high priest. And Simon Peter stood and warmed himself. They said therefore unto him, Art not thou also one of his disciples? He denied it, and said, I am not. One of the servants of the high priest, being his kinsman whose ear Peter cut off, saith, Did not I see thee in the garden with him? Peter then denied again: and immediately the cock crew.

5. Meditation: Miserere, my Maker

Anon., c.1615

Miserere, my Maker,
O have mercy on me, wretch, strangely distressèd,
Cast down with sin oppressèd;
Mightily vexed to the soul's bitter anguish,
E'en to the death I languish.
Yet let it please Thee
To hear my ceaseless crying:
Miserere, miserere, I am dying.

T0056736

Miserere, my Saviour,
I, alas, am for my sins fearfully grievèd,
And cannot be relievèd
But by Thy death, which Thou didst suffer for me,
Wherefore I adore Thee.
And do beseech Thee
To hear my ceaseless crying:
Miserere, miserere, I am dying.

Holy Spirit, miserere,
Comfort my distressèd soul, grieved for youth's folly,
Purge, cleanse and make it holy;
With Thy sweet due of grace and peace inspire me,
How I desire Thee.
And strengthen me now
In this, my ceaseless crying:
Miserere, miserere, I am dying.

6. Hymn: Drop, drop, slow tears

Music: Bob Chilcott; Words: Phineas Fletcher (1582–1650)

SHERLAW-JOHNSON

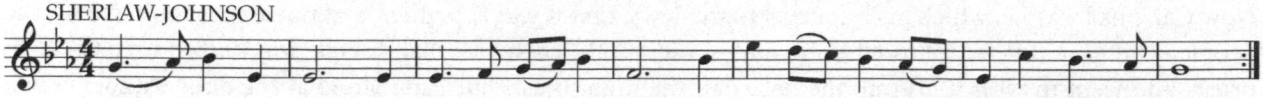

© Oxford University Press 2013

1. Drop, drop, slow tears,
   And bathe those beauteous feet,
   Which brought from heav'n
   The news and Prince of Peace.

2. Cease not, wet eyes,
   His mercies to entreat;
   To cry for vengeance
   Sin doth never cease.

3. In your deep floods
   Drown all my faults and fears;
   Nor let his eye
   See sin, but through my tears.

7. The Judgment Hall (I)

John 18: 28–36

Then led they Jesus from Caiaphas unto the hall of judgment: and it was early; and they themselves went not into the judgment hall, lest they should be defiled; but that they might eat the passover. Pilate then went out unto them, and said, What accusation bring ye against this man? They answered and said unto him, If he were not a malefactor, we would not have delivered him up unto thee. Then said Pilate unto them, Take ye him, and judge him according to your law. The Jews therefore said unto him, It is not lawful for us to put any man to death: That the saying of Jesus might be fulfilled, which he spake, signifying what death he should die. Then Pilate entered into the judgment hall again, and called Jesus, and said unto him, Art thou the King of the Jews? Jesus answered him, Sayest thou this thing of thyself, or did others tell it thee of me? Pilate answered, Am I a Jew? Thine own nation and the chief priests have delivered thee unto me: what hast thou done? Jesus answered, My kingdom is not of this world: if my kingdom were of this world, then would my servants fight, that I should not be delivered to the Jews: but now is my kingdom not from hence.

8. Hymn: Jesu, grant me this, I pray

Music: Bob Chilcott; Words: 17th-century Latin, trans. Sir Henry Williams Baker (1821–77)

WITHAMS

© Oxford University Press 2013

1. Jesu, grant me this, I pray,
   Ever in thy heart to stay;
   Let me evermore abide
   Hidden in thy wounded side.

2. If the evil one prepare,
   Or the world, a tempting snare,
   I am safe when I abide
   In thy heart and wounded side.

3. If the flesh, more dangerous still,
   Tempt my soul to deeds of ill,
   Naught I fear when I abide
   In thy heart and wounded side.

4. Death will come one day to me;
   Jesu, cast me not from thee:
   Dying let me still abide
   In thy heart and wounded side.

9. Meditation: Christ, my Beloved

William Baldwin (d. c.1563)

Christ, my Beloved which still doth feed
Among the flowers, having delight
Among his faithful lilies,
Doth take great care for me indeed,
And I again with all my might
Will do what so his will is.

My Love in me and I in him,
Conjoined by love, will still abide
Among the faithful lilies
Till day do break, and truth do dim
All shadows dark and cause them slide,
According as his will is.

10. The Judgment Hall (II)

John 18: 37–19: 11

Pilate therefore said unto him, Art thou a king then? Jesus answered, Thou sayest that I am a king. To this end was I born, and for this cause came I into the world, that I should bear witness unto the truth. Every one that is of the truth heareth my voice. Pilate saith unto him, What is truth? And when he said this, he went out again unto the Jews, and saith unto them, I find in him no fault at all. But ye have a custom, that I should release unto you one at the passover: will ye therefore that I release unto you the King of the Jews? Then cried they all again, saying, Not this man, but Barabbas. Now Barabbas was a robber. Then Pilate therefore took Jesus, and scourged him. And the soldiers platted a crown of thorns, and put it on his head, and they put on him a purple robe, And said, Hail, King of the Jews! And they smote him with their hands. Pilate therefore went forth again, and saith unto them, Behold, I bring him forth to you, that ye may know that I find no fault in him. Then came Jesus forth, wearing the crown of thorns, and the purple robe, And Pilate saith unto them, Behold the man! When the chief priests therefore and officers saw him, they cried out, saying, Crucify him, crucify him. Pilate saith unto them, Take ye him, and crucify him: for I find no fault in him. The Jews answered him, We have a law, and by our law he ought to die, because he made himself the Son of God. When Pilate therefore heard that saying, he was the more afraid; And went again into the judgment hall, and saith unto Jesus, Whence art thou? But Jesus gave him no answer. Then saith Pilate unto him, Speakest thou not unto me? Knowest thou not that I have power to crucify thee, and have power to release thee? Jesus answered, Thou couldest have no power at all against me, except it were given thee from above: therefore he that delivered me unto thee hath the greater sin.

11. Meditation: Away vain world

Alexander Montgomerie (?1545–?1610), modernized and adapted by Bob Chilcott

Away vain world, bewitcher of my heart!
My sorrow shows, my sin makes me to smart!
Yet will I not despair
But to my God repair,
He has mercy ay,
Therefore will I pray.
He has mercy ay and loves me
Though by his humbling hand he proves me.

Once more away, shows loth[1] the world to leave,
Bids oft adieu with it that holds me slave.
Loth am I to forgo
This sweet alluring foe.
Since thy ways are vain,
Shall I thee retain?
Since thy ways are vain, I quite[2] thee.
Thy pleasures shall no more delight me.

What shall I say? Are all my pleasures past?
Shall worldly joys now take their leave at last?
Yea, Christ, these earthly toys
Shall turn in heavenly joys.
Let the world be gone,
I'll love Christ alone!
Let the world be gone, I care not.
Christ is my love alone, I fear not.

[1] loth = loath/unwilling
[2] quite = quit/leave

12. Jesus is Crucified

John 19: 12–22

And from thenceforth Pilate sought to release him: but the Jews cried out, saying, If thou let this man go, thou art not Caesar's friend: whosoever maketh himself a king speaketh against Caesar. When Pilate therefore heard that saying, he brought Jesus forth, and sat down in the judgment seat in a place that is called the Pavement, but in the Hebrew, Gabbatha. And it was the preparation of the passover, and about the sixth hour: and he saith unto the Jews, Behold your King! But they cried out, Away with him, away with him, crucify him. Pilate saith unto them, Shall I crucify your King? The chief priests answered, We have no king but Caesar. Then delivered he him therefore unto them to be crucified. And they took Jesus, and led him away. And he bearing his cross went forth into a place called the place of a skull, which is called in the Hebrew Golgotha: Where they crucified him, and two other with him, on either side one, and Jesus in the midst. And Pilate wrote a title, and put it on the cross. And the writing was, JESUS OF NAZARETH THE KING OF THE JEWS. This title then read many of the Jews: for the place where Jesus was crucified was nigh to the city: and it was written in Hebrew, and Greek, and Latin. Then said the chief priests of the Jews to Pilate, Write not, The King of the Jews; but that he said, I am King of the Jews. Pilate answered, What I have written I have written.

13. Hymn: There is a green hill far away

Music: Bob Chilcott; Words: Mrs Cecil Frances Alexander (1818–95)

© Oxford University Press 2013

1. There is a green hill far away,
   Without a city wall,
   Where the dear Lord was crucified,
   Who died to save us all,
   Who died to save us all.

2. We may not know, we cannot tell,
   What pains he had to bear,
   But we believe it was for us
   He hung and suffered there,
   He hung and suffered there.

3. He died that we might be forgiv'n,
   He died to make us good,
   That we might go at last to heav'n,
   Saved by his precious blood,
   Saved by his precious blood.

4. O dearly, dearly has he loved,
   And we must love him too,
   And trust in his redeeming blood,
   And try his works to do,
   And try his works to do.

14. The Crucifixion

John 19: 23–7

Then the soldiers, when they had crucified Jesus, took his garments, and made four parts, to every soldier a part; and also his coat: now the coat was without seam, woven from the top throughout. They said therefore among themselves, Let us not rend it, but cast lots for it, whose it shall be: That the scripture might be fulfilled, which saith, They parted my raiment among them, and for my vesture they did cast lots. These things therefore the soldiers did. Now there stood by the cross of Jesus his mother, and his mother's sister, Mary the wife of Cleophas, and Mary Magdalene. When Jesus therefore saw his mother, and the disciple standing by, whom he loved, he saith unto his mother, Woman, behold thy son! Then saith he to the disciple, Behold thy mother!

15. Meditation: Jesus, my Leman

13th-century English, adapted by Bob Chilcott

When I see upon the Cross
Jesus, my leman[1],
And by him standing Mary and Johan,
With his back scourged
And his side pierced,
For the love of man,
Well ought I to weep
And sins relinquish,
If I know of love.

[1] leman = loved one

16. Jesus Dies on the Cross

John 19: 28–30

After this, Jesus knowing that all things were now accomplished, that the scripture might be fulfilled, saith, I thirst. Now there was set a vessel full of vinegar; and they filled a sponge with vinegar, and put it upon hyssop, and put it to his mouth. When Jesus had received the vinegar, he said, It is finished. And he bowed his head, and gave up the ghost.

17. Hymn: When I survey the Wondrous Cross

Music: Bob Chilcott; Words: Isaac Watts (1674–1748)

© Oxford University Press 2013

1. When I survey the Wondrous Cross,
   On which the Prince of glory died,
   My richest gain I count but loss,
   And pour contempt on all my pride,
   And pour contempt on all my pride.

2. Forbid it, Lord, that I should boast,
   Save in the death of Christ my God;
   All the vain things that charm me most,
   I sacrifice them to his blood,
   I sacrifice them to his blood.

3. See from his head, his hands, his feet,
   Sorrow and love flow mingled down;
   Did e'er such love and sorrow meet,
   Or thorns compose so rich a crown,
   Or thorns compose so rich a crown?

4. Were the whole realm of nature mine,
   That were a present far too small;
   Love so amazing, so divine,
   Demands my soul, my life, my all,
   Demands my soul, my life, my all.

St John Passion

to A. C. F.

ST JOHN PASSION

PART 1

1. Sing, my tongue, the glorious battle

Bishop Venantius Fortunatus (*c.*530–*c.*600)
trans. Percy Dearmer (1867–1936)

BOB CHILCOTT

© Oxford University Press 2013

Printed in Great Britain

OXFORD UNIVERSITY PRESS, MUSIC DEPARTMENT, GREAT CLARENDON STREET, OXFORD OX2 6DP
The Moral Rights of the Composer have been asserted. Photocopying this copyright material is ILLEGAL.

9
f
Now a - bove the Cross, the tro - phy, Sound the loud tri - um - phant lay:
When he fell on death by tast - ing Fruit of the for - bid - den tree;
13
ff
f
Tell how Christ, the world's Re - deem - er, As a vic - tim won the
Then an - o - ther tree was cho - sen Which the world from death should
17a
1.
2.
ff
day.
free.
f

2. The Garden

John 18: 1, 3–13

© Oxford University Press 2013. Photocopying this copyright material is ILLEGAL.

14
cresc.
f
slowing
thi - ther with lan - terns and tor - ches and wea - pons.
cresc.
f
calmer
17
mp
3
Je - sus there - fore, know - ing all things that should come u - pon him, went
mp
more agitated
19
p
JESUS
p
EVANGELIST
mf
forth, and said un - to them, Whom seek ye? They an - swered him,
p
mf
Ped.
Man.
23
f
Je - sus of Na - za - reth,
S.
A.
Je - sus of Na - za - reth, Je - sus, Je - sus,
Je - sus of Na - za - reth.
f
T.
B.
Je - sus, Je - sus of Na - za - reth, Je - sus,
f
Ped.

calmer
EVANGELIST
JESUS
more agitated
EVANGELIST
27
mp
p
p
mf
Je - sus saith un - to them, I am he. And Ju - das al - so, which be -
mp
p
mf
Man.
Ped.
Man.
31
- trayed him, stood with them. And soon then as he had said un - to them, I am
33
f
slowing
mp
he, they went back - ward, and fell to the ground. Then
f
calmer
JESUS
more agitated
EVANGELIST
36
p
p
mf
asked he them a - gain, Whom seek ye? And they said,
p
mf
Ped.
Man.

40
S.
A.
Je - sus of Na - za - reth,
Je - sus of Na - za - reth, Je - sus, Je - sus,
Je - sus of Na - za - reth.
T.
B.
Je - sus, Je - sus of Na - za - reth, Je - sus,
Ped.
44
calmer
EVANGELIST
JESUS
Je - sus an - swered, I have told you that I am
Man.
Ped.
47
EVANGELIST
he: if there - fore ye seek me, let these go their way: That the
51
say - ing might be ful - filled, which he spake, Of them which thou ga - vest me have I lost
Man.

more agitated
54
f
none. Then Si - mon Pe - ter hav - ing a sword drew it, and
57
smote the high priest's ser - vant, and cut off his right ear.
59
calmer
mf
mp
The ser - vant's name was Mal - chus. Then said Je - sus un - to
62
JESUS
mp
Pe - ter, Put up thy sword in - to the sheath: the cup which my
Ped.

more agitated
EVANGELIST
65
mf
Fa - ther hath gi - ven me, shall I not drink it, drink it? Then the
68
f
band and the cap - tain and of - fi - cers of the Jews took Je - sus, and
Man.
70
mf
bound him, And led him a - way to An - nas first; for he was the fa - ther in
mp
73
poco rit.
law to Ca - ia - phas, which was the high priest that same year.

3. Hymn: It is a thing most wonderful

Bishop William Walsham How (1823–97)

'ELTON'

© Oxford University Press 2013. Photocopying this copyright material is ILLEGAL.

DESCANT SOPRANOS
22
f
3. It is most won - der - ful to know His
ALL OTHER VOICES
f
3. It is most won - der - ful to know His love for
cresc.
f
30
love for me so free and sure; But 'tis more won - der -
me so free and sure; But 'tis more won - der - ful to
36
poco rit.
- ful to see My love for him so faint and poor.
see My love for him so faint, so faint and poor.
poco rit.

4. *Peter's Denial*

John 18: 14–27

© Oxford University Press 2013. Photocopying this copyright material is ILLEGAL.

10
f
mp espress.
pa - lace of the high priest. But Pe - ter stood at the
f
mp espress.
12
mf
door with - out. Then went out that o - ther dis - ci - ple, which was
mf
14
known un - to the high priest, and spake un - to her that kept the door, and
16
brought in Pe - ter. Then saith the dam - sel that kept the door un - to
WOMAN (SOPRANO)
EVANGELIST
18
f
Pe - ter, Art not thou al - so one of this man's dis - ci - ples? He
f
f

21
PETER (TENOR)
f
mf EVANGELIST
saith, I am not. And the ser-vants and of - fi - cers stood there, who had
mf
24
f
mf
made a fire of coals; for it was cold: and they warmed them-selves:
f
mf
27
mp
mf
and Pe - ter stood with them, and warmed him - self. The
mp
29
high priest then asked Je - sus of his dis - ci - ples, and of his doc - trine.
mf
poco rit.
Slower ♩ = c.60
31
mp
JESUS
mp
Je - sus an - swered him, I spake o - pen - ly to the
f
mp
mp
Ped.

34
mf
world; I ev - er taught in the sy - na - gogue, and in the tem - ple,
mf
37
mp
whi - ther the Jews al - ways re - sort; and in se - cret have I said no - thing. Why
mp
mp
40
mf cresc.
ask - est thou me? Ask them which heard me, what I have said un - to them: be -
mf cresc.
f
Tempo I (♩ = c.84)
EVANGELIST
43
mf
- hold, they know what I said. And when he had thus spo - ken, one of the
f
mf
Man.

46
f
of - fi - cers which stood by struck Je - sus with the palm of his hand, say - ing,
48
OFFICER (TENOR)
f
An - swer-est thou the high priest so?
EVANGELIST
mp
poco rit.
Je - sus an - swered him,
mp
Tempo II (♩ = c. 60)
JESUS
52
mp
mf
If I have spo - ken e - vil, bear wit - ness of the e - vil: but if well, why smi - test thou
mf
Ped.
Tempo I (♩ = c. 84)
55
EVANGELIST
mf
me?
Now An - nas had sent him bound un - to
Man.

57
Ca - ia - phas the high priest. And Si - mon Pe - ter stood and warmed him - self.
60
S.
A.
Art not thou al - so one of his dis -
(EVANGELIST)
T.
B.
They said there - fore un - to him,
Ped.
62
not one of his dis - ci - ples, dis - ci - ples?
- ci - ples, not one of his dis - ci - ples, one of his dis - ci - ples?
one of his dis - ci - ples, one of his dis - ci - ples?
- ci - ples, art not thou al - so one of his dis - ci - ples, dis - ci - ples?

64
EVANGELIST
f
He de - nied it, and said,
PETER (TENOR)
f
I am not.
Man.
67
EVANGELIST
mf
One of the ser - vants of the high priest, be - ing his kins - man whose ear Pe - ter cut off,
mf
69
f
SERVANT (TENOR)
mf
saith, Did not I see thee in the gar - den with him?
poco rit.
Tempo II (♩ = c. 60)
EVANGELIST
mp
Pe - ter then de - nied a -
f mf
mp
73
mf espress.
rit.
p
- gain: and im - me - diate - ly, im - me - diate - ly the cock crew.
mf espress.
p
Ped.

5. Meditation: Miserere, my Maker

Anon., *c.*1615

© Oxford University Press 2013. Photocopying this copyright material is ILLEGAL.

13
Cast down with sin op - press - ed; Might - i - ly vexed to the
- re - - re,
- re - - re, Cast down with sin, with sin op -
- re - - re, Cast down with sin op - press - ed; the
- re - re, Cast down with sin op - press - ed; the

19
mf ma dolce
soul's bit - ter an - guish, E'en to the death I lan - guish. Yet let it
- press - ed; the soul's an - guish, to the death I lan - guish, it
soul's bit - ter an - guish, E'en to the death, it
soul's bit - ter an - guish, to the death, it

25
mp
please Thee To hear my cease - less cry - ing: Mi - se -
please, it please Thee To hear my cry - - ing:
please Thee To hear, to hear my cry - - ing:
please Thee To hear my cease - less cry - - ing:
mp
31
p
- re - re, mi - se - re - re, I am dy - ing.
mp
p
mi - se - re - re, mi - se - re - - re.
Mi - se - re - re, mi - - - - se - re - re.
mp
p
mp
Mi - se - re - re, mi - se - re - - re. Mi - se -
mp
p
Mi - se - re - re, mi - - se - - re - - re.
mp
p

37
mp
My Sa - viour, mi - se - re - re,
mi - se -
mp
Mi - se - re - re, my Sa - viour, mi - se -
mf ma dolce
- re - re, my Sa - viour, I, a - las, am for my sins
mp
Mi - - - - se - re - - - re, mi - se - re - re, my
mp

42
p cresc.
mi - se - re - - re, mi - se - re - re, And can - not
- re - re, mi - se - re - re, mi - se - re - - re,
p cresc.
- re - re, mi - - - se - re - re, can - not be re -
mp cresc.
fear - ful - ly griev - ed, And can-not be re -
mi - - - se - re - - re,
p cresc.
Sa - viour, mi - - se - - re - - re, can - not
p cresc.

48
mp cresc.
be re - liev - ed, by Thy death, which Thou didst suf - fer for
mp cresc.
- liev - ed, by Thy death, which Thou didst suf - fer for
mf cresc.
- liev - ed But by Thy death, which Thou didst suf - fer for
mp cresc.
be re - liev - - ed, by Thy death Thou didst suf - fer for
mp cresc.

54
mf ma dolce
me, Where - fore I a - dore Thee. And do be - seech Thee To hear my
mf ma dolce
me, Where - fore I a - dore Thee. And do be - seech, be - seech Thee To
f mf ma dolce
me, Where - fore I a - dore Thee. And do be - seech Thee To hear, to
mf ma dolce
me, Where - fore I do be - seech Thee To hear my
mf ma dolce

60
mp
p
cease - less cry - ing: Mi - se - re - re, mi - se - re - re, I am dy - ing.
mp
p
mi - se -
hear my cry - - ing: Mi - se - re - re, mi - -
mp
p
hear my cry - - ing: Mi - se - re - re, mi - se -
mp
p
cease - less cry - - ing: Mi - se - re - re, mi - -
mp
p

66
pp
- re - re, mi - se - re - re.
Ho - ly Spi - rit, mi - se - re - re, Com-fort my dis-tress - ed
pp
- - se - re - re.
Ho - ly Spi - rit, mi - se - re - re, Com - fort
pp
- - re - - re.
Ho - ly Spi - rit, mi - se - re - re, Com - fort,
pp
- se - - re - - re.
Ho - ly Spi - rit, mi - se - re - re, Com - fort
pp

72
soul, grieved for youth's fol - ly,
mi - se - re - re, mi - se - re -
my dis - tress - ed soul, mi - - - se - re -
com - fort my dis - tress - ed soul, mi - - - se - re -
my dis - tress - ed soul, mi - - se - - re -

78
Purge, cleanse and make it ho - ly; With Thy sweet due of grace and
- re,
- re, Purge, cleanse and make it ho - ly; With Thy sweet due of grace and
- re, Purge, cleanse and make it ho - ly; With Thy sweet due of grace and
- re, Purge, cleanse and make it ho - ly; Thy sweet due of grace and

84
p (mp)
peace in - spire me, How I de - sire Thee. And strength-en me
p (mp)
peace in - spire me, How I de - sire Thee. And strength-en me
p (mp)
peace in - spire me, How I de - sire Thee. And strength-en me
p (mp)
peace in - spire me, How I de - sire Thee. And strength-en me
p (mp)

90
now In this, my cease - less cry - ing: Mi - se - re - re, mi - se -
now In this, my cease - less cry - - ing: Mi - se -
now In this, my cease - less cry - - ing: Mi - se -
now In this, my cease - less cry - - ing: Mi - se - re -

96a
1.
2.
p
-re - re, I am dy - ing, -re - re, I am dy - ing,
mi - se - re - re, mi - se -
-re - re, I am dy - ing, -re - re, mi - se -
-re, I am dy - ing, -re, mi - se -
99
rit.
pp
am dy - ing, dy - ing.
-re - re, mi - se - re - re, mi - se - re - re.
-re - re, mi - se - re - re.
-re - re, mi - se - re - re.
-re - re, mi - se - re - re.

6. Hymn: Drop, drop, slow tears

Phineas Fletcher (1582–1650)

'SHERLAW-JOHNSON'

*Melody by Orlando Gibbons (1583–1625)

© Oxford University Press 2013. Photocopying this copyright material is ILLEGAL.

PART 2

7. The Judgment Hall (I)

John 18: 28–36

© Oxford University Press 2013. Photocopying this copyright material is ILLEGAL.

12
PILATE
EVANGELIST
them, and said, What ac - cu - sa - tion bring ye a - gainst this man? They
15
S.
A.
T.
B.
If he were not a ma - le - fac - tor,
(EVANGELIST)
an - swered and said un - to him,
ff marcato
Ped.
17
we would not have de - li - vered him up un - to thee, up un - to thee.

20
EVANGELIST
f
Then said Pi - late un - to them,
PILATE
f
Take ye him, and
f
Man.
23
S.
ff
A.
It
T.
B.
ff
(PILATE)
judge him ac - cord - ing to your law.
EVANGELIST
f
The Jews there - fore said un - to him,
Ped.
25
is not law - ful for us, for us to put a - ny man to death:
ff marcato

28
EVANGELIST
mf
That the say - ing of Je - sus might be ful -
sub. mf marcato
Man.
31
f
- filled, which he spake, sig - ni - fy - ing what death he should die. Then
34
Pi - late en - tered in - to the judg-ment hall a - gain, and called Je - sus, and said un - to
f
37
PILATE
f
him, Art thou the King of the Jews?
EVANGELIST
mf
Je - sus an-swered him,
slowing
mf

calmer
JESUS
mp espress.
41
Say - est thou this thing of thy - self, or did o - thers tell it thee of
mp espress.
Ped.
more agitated
EVANGELIST
PILATE
45
mf
f
me?
Pi - late an - swered,
Am I a Jew? Thine own
mf
f
Man.
49
na - tion and the chief priests have de - li - vered thee un - to me:
slowing
EVANGELIST
51
mf
what hast thou done?
Je - sus an - swered,
mf

calmer
JESUS
mp espress.
My king - dom is not of this world: if my
mp espress.
Ped.
mf
king - dom were of this world, then would my ser - vants fight,
mf
f
f
mf
that I should not be de - li - vered to the Jews:
mf
rit.
mp
but now is my king - dom not from hence.
mp
p
p

8. Hymn: Jesu, grant me this, I pray

17th-century Latin
trans. Sir Henry Williams Baker (1821–77)

'WITHAMS'

© Oxford University Press 2013. Photocopying this copyright material is ILLEGAL.

DESCANT SOPRANOS
11
f
4. Death will come one day to me; Je - su, cast me
ALL OTHER VOICES unis.
f
f
14
not from thee: Dy - ing let me still a - bide
rit.
17
In thy heart and wound - ed side.
rit.

9. Meditation: Christ, my Beloved

William Baldwin (d. *c.*1563)

© Oxford University Press 2013. Photocopying this copyright material is ILLEGAL.

14
p cresc. espress.
Doth take great care for me in - deed, And I a - gain with
p cresc. espress.
18
f
mp
all my might Will do what so his will is, will do what so his will is,
f
mp
22
p
what his will is.
p
mp
Man.
26
mp
My
p
mp
Ped.

30
(SOPRANO SOLO)
Love in me and I in him, Con-joined by love, will still a-bide A-
S.
p
Love in me, I in him, a - bide a -
A.
p
Love in me, I in him, love will a - bide a -
T.
p
Love in him, Con - joined, will still a - bide
B.
p
Love, love a -
34
-mong the faith-ful li - lies, a - mong the faith-ful li - lies
p cresc.
-mong the li - lies, faith - ful li - lies Till
p cresc.
-mong the li - lies, faith - ful li - lies Till
p cresc.
a - mong the li - lies, faith - ful li - lies Till
p cresc.
-mong the li - - lies Till

37
mp cresc.
f
Till day do break, do break, and
espress.
f
day do break, and truth do dim All sha - dows dark and cause them slide,
cause them slide,
espress.
f
day do break, All sha - dows dark and cause them slide, them
espress.
f
day do break, All sha - dows dark and cause them slide,
espress.
f
day do break, All sha - dows dark and cause them
p cresc. espress.
f
Ped.
41
mp
truth do dim, and truth do dim.
mp
Ac - cord-ing as his will is, ac - cord-ing as his will is, as his
mp
slide, Ac - cord - ing as, ac - cord - ing as his will is,
mp
slide, Ac - cord-ing as his will is, ac - cord - ing as his will is,
mp
slide, Ac - cord - ing, ac - cord - ing as his
mp

45
p
will is.
p
will is.
p
will is.
p
will is.
p
mp
p
Man.
Ped.
50
rit.
p
pp
Christ, my Be - lov - ed.
p
pp
My Be - lov - ed.
p
pp
My Be - lov - ed.
p
pp
My Be - lov - ed.
p
pp
My Be - lov - ed.
rit.
mp
p
pp

10. The Judgment Hall (II)

John 18: 37–19: 11

© Oxford University Press 2013. Photocopying this copyright material is ILLEGAL.

17
truth.
Ev - 'ry one that is of the truth
3
22
mf
hear - eth my voice.
EVANGELIST
mf
Pi - late
mf
Man.
26
saith un - to him,
PILATE
f
What is truth?
f
EVANGELIST
mf
And
mf
30
when he had said this, he went out a - gain un - to the Jews,
f
and saith un - to
f

33
PILATE
f
them, I find in him no fault at all. But ye have a cus - tom, that
37
I should re - lease un - to you one at the pass - o - ver: will ye there - fore that I re -
41
EVANGELIST
f
- lease un - to you the King of the Jews? Then cried they all a - gain,
44
S.
ff
Ba - rab - bas,
A.
Not this man, but
Ba - rab - bas, not
Ba - rab - bas,
(EVANGELIST)
T.
say - ing,
B.
ff
Ba - rab - bas, not
ff
Ped.

47
this man, but Ba - rab - bas, Ba - rab - bas.
EVANGELIST
f
Now
f
Man.
50
3
3
mf
3
Ba - rab - bas was a rob - ber. Then Pi - late there - fore took Je - sus, and
mf
54
f
scourged him, and scourged him.
f
58
mf
3
And the sol - diers plat - ted a crown of thorns, and
mf marcato

62
put it on his head, and they put on him a pur - ple robe, And said,
66
S.
A.
Hail, King of the Jews, King of the Jews!
T.
B.
Ped.
70
EVANGELIST
And they smote him with their hands.
Pi - late there-fore went forth a- gain, and
marcato
Man.
73
PILATE
saith un - to them,
Be - hold, I bring him forth to

76
EVANGELIST
f appass.
you, that ye may know that I find no fault in him. Then came
f appass.
80
Je - sus forth, Je - sus forth, wear - ing the crown of thorns, and the
84
mf
PILATE
mf
pur - ple robe, And Pi - late saith un - to them, Be-hold the
mf
89
f appass.
EVANGELIST
mf
man!
When the
f appass.
mf

94
chief priests there-fore and of-fi-cers saw him, they cried out, say-ing,
98
S.
A.
Cru-ci-fy him, cru-ci-fy him, cru-ci-fy him.
T.
B.
Ped.
EVANGELIST
PILATE
102
Pi-late saith un-to them, Take ye him, and cru-ci-fy him: for I
Man.
107
find no fault in him.
f appass.
EVANGELIST
The Jews

112
ff
S.
A.
We have a law, and by our law he
(EVANGELIST)
T.
an - swered him,
B.
ff
ff
Ped.
115
ought to die, be - cause he made him - self the Son of
118
fff
God.
fff
fff
ff
f dim.

123
mf dim.
128
EVANGELIST
mp
When Pi - late there-fore heard that say - ing, he was the
mp
Man.
133
mf
more a - fraid; And went a - gain in - to the judg - ment hall, and saith un - to
mf
137
PILATE
f
Je - sus, Whence art thou?
f
EVANGELIST
mp
But Je - sus gave him no an - swer.
mp
142
mf
Then saith Pi - late un - to him,
mf
PILATE
f
Speak-est thou not un - to
f

146
me? Know-est thou not that I have pow'r to cru-ci-fy thee, and have pow'r to re-lease thee?
poco rit.
Slower ♩ = c. 54
151
EVANGELIST
mf
JESUS
mp espress.
Je - sus an-swered, Thou could-est have no pow'r at all a-gainst me,
mf
mp espress.
Ped.
156
ex - cept it were gi - ven thee from a - bove: there - fore
161
mf
rit.
dim.
p
he that de - li-vered me un - to thee hath the great - er sin.
mf
dim.
p

11. Meditation: Away vain world

Alexander Montgomerie (?1545–?1610)
modernized BC

© Oxford University Press 2013. Photocopying this copyright material is ILLEGAL.

8
to my God re - pair, He has mer - cy ay, There - fore will I pray.
God re - pair, He has mer - cy ay, will I pray.
to my God re - pair, He has mer - cy ay, There - fore will I pray.
God re - pair, He has mer - cy ay, will I pray.
11
mp p pp
He has mer - cy ay and loves me Though by his hum - bling hand he proves me.
A - way,
Mer - cy, and loves me, by his hand. A - way, a -
He has mer - cy ay and loves me, by his hand. A - way, a -
Mer - cy, and loves me, by his hand. A - way,

**loth* = loath/unwilling

**quite* = quit/leave

29
p dolce
shall I___ say? Are all my plea-sures past? Shall world-ly___ joys now take their leave at last?___ Yea,
a - way, a - way,_ a - way, a - way, a - way,_ a - way,___ Yea,
a - way, a - way, a - way,___ a - way, a - way, a - way,___ Yea,
a - way, a - - way, a - way, a - way,___ Yea,

33
Christ, these earth-ly toys Shall turn in heav'n-ly joys. Let the world be gone, I'll love_ Christ a-lone!
Christ, these earth-ly toys___ in heav'n - ly joys.___ Let the world be gone,_ I'll love_ Christ a-lone!
Christ, these earth-ly toys Shall turn in heav'n-ly joys. Let the world be gone, I'll love_ Christ a - lone!___
Christ, these earth-ly toys in heav'n - ly joys. Let the world be gone, I'll love Christ a-lone!

37
mp (f)
p (mp)
mf
Let the world be gone, I care not. Christ is my love a - lone, I fear not. Yea,
Gone, I care not. Christ a - lone, I fear not. Yea,
Let the world be gone, I care not. Christ a - lone, I fear, fear not. Yea,
Gone, I care not. Christ a - lone, I fear not. Yea,
40b
dim.
rit.
pp
fear not, I fear not, I fear not.
fear, I fear not, I fear not.
fear not, fear not.
fear not, fear not, fear not.
fear not, fear not, fear not.

PART 3

12. Jesus is Crucified

John 19: 12–22

© Oxford University Press 2013. Photocopying this copyright material is ILLEGAL.

8
who - so - ev - er ma - keth him - self a king speak - eth a - gainst Cae - sar.

EVANGELIST
11
When Pi - late there-fore heard that say - ing, he brought Je - sus forth, and sat down in the

14
judg-ment seat in a place that is called the Pave - ment, but in the He - brew, Gab - ba - tha. And
Man.

17
it was the pre - pa - ra - tion of the pass - o - ver, and a - bout the sixth
Ped.
19
ff
S.
A.
A -
hour: and he saith un - to the Jews,
PILATE
f
Be - hold your King!
EVANGELIST
f
But they cried out, A -
ff
T.
B.
ff
f
22
- way with him, cru - ci - fy, a - way with him, cru - ci - fy him.
- way, a - way with him, cru - ci - fy, a - way with him, cru - ci - fy him.
ff

*The bracketed section may be performed by a solo cellist. See p. 82 for a separate cello part.

36
rit.
f
p
mp
p
mp
Soft and with simplicity ♩ = c.58
EVANGELIST
40
p
Then de - li - vered he him there - fore un - to them to be
p dolce
43
mp
p dolce
cru - ci - fied. And they took Je - sus, and led him a - way. And he
mp
46
bear - ing his cross went forth in - to a place called the place of a skull, which is
p dolce
49
called in the He - brew Gol - go - tha: Where they cru - ci - fied him, and

52
two o - ther with him, on ei - ther side one, and Je - sus in the midst. And
55
Pi - late wrote a ti - tle, and put it on the cross. And the writ - ing was,
58
JE - SUS OF NA - ZA - RETH THE KING OF THE JEWS. This
a little quicker
61
mp
ti - tle then read ma - ny of the Jews: for the place where Je - sus was cru - ci - fied was
mp

64
nigh to the ci - ty: and it was writ - ten in He - brew, and Greek, and
66
La - tin. Then said the chief priests of the Jews to Pi - late,
69
S.
A.
f
ff
Write not, The King of the Jews; but that he said, I am King of the Jews.
T.
B.
f
ff
f
ff
Ped.
72
EVANGELIST
mf
Pi - late an - swered,
PILATE
mf
What I have writ - ten I have writ - ten.
mf
Man.

in loving memory P. S. L.

13. Hymn: There is a green hill far away

Mrs Cecil Frances Alexander (1818–95)

'LEDGER'

© Oxford University Press 2013. Photocopying this copyright material is ILLEGAL.

16
But we be - lieve it was for us He hung and suf - fered there,
But we be - lieve it was for us He hung and suf - fered there, he
20
suf - - fered there.
hung and suf - fered there.
p
3. He died that we might
p
p
23
be for - giv'n, He died to make us good, That we might go at
be for - giv'n, He died to make us good, That we might go at
27
last to heav'n, Saved by his pre - cious blood,
last to heav'n, Saved by his pre - cious blood, saved by his pre - cious

DESCANT SOPRANOS
31
f
4. O dear - ly has he loved, And we must
blood.
ALL OTHER VOICES
f
4. O dear-ly, dear - ly has he loved, And we must love him
mp
f
Ped.
35
love him too, And trust in his re - deem - ing
too, And trust in his re - deem - ing blood, And
38
rit.
blood, And try his works to do, and try his works to do.
try his works to do, and try his works to do.
rit.

14. The Crucifixion

John 19: 23–7

© Oxford University Press 2013. Photocopying this copyright material is ILLEGAL.

16
mp
coat: now the coat was with - out seam, wo - ven from the top through-
mp
19
p
- out. They said there - fore a - mong them - selves,
p
22
S.
A.
mp
mf
3
3
p
Let us not rend it, but cast lots for it, whose it shall be:
EVANGELIST
p
3
T.
B.
mp
mf
3
3
p
That the
mp
p
Ped.
25
mf
3
3
3
scrip - ture might be ful - filled, which saith, They part - ed my rai - ment a -
(cello solo)
p
mf
Man.

27
- mong them, and for my ves - ture they did cast lots.
These things there-fore the sol - diers did.
p
mf
mp
29
p dolce
Now there stood by the cross of Je - sus his mo - ther, and his
p dolce
32
mo - ther's sis - ter, Ma - ry the wife of Cle - o - phas, and
34
Ma - ry Mag - da - le - ne.
When Je - sus there - fore saw his

36
mo-ther, and the dis-ci - ple stand-ing by, whom he loved, he saith un - to his mo-ther,
JESUS
EVANGELIST
39
mp espress.
Wo - man, wo - - man, be - hold thy son!
p
Then
mp espress.
Ped.
JESUS
mp espress.
42
saith he to the dis - ci - ple,
Be - hold, be - hold thy
p
mp espress.
Man.
Ped.
45
dim.
p
mo-ther, thy mo-ther, mo-ther!
p

15. Meditation: Jesus, my Leman

13th-century English
adap. BC

*leman = loved one

© Oxford University Press 2013. Photocopying this copyright material is ILLEGAL.

16
a tempo
mp cresc.
mf
know of love, I know of love, if I know of love, I know of love,
p cresc.
mp cresc.
mf
20
mp
p
if I know of love.
mp
p
Man.
25
p espress.
S.
A.
When I see u - pon the Cross Je - sus, my le - man,
T.
B.
p espress.
When u - pon the Cross Je - sus, my le - man,
mp
29
And by him stand - ing
mp cresc.
By him stand - ing Ma - ry and Jo - han,
With his back scourged And his
By him Ma - ry and Jo - han,
mp cresc.
mp cresc.
Ped.

32
S.
mf
side pierced, For the love of man, Well ought I to weep And
A.
mf
side pierced, Love of man, Well ought I to weep
T.
mf
side pierced, For the love of man, Well ought I to weep
B.
mf
side pierced, Love of man, Well ought I to weep
mf
35
mp
poco rit.
a tempo
p cresc.
sins re - lin - quish, If I know of love, I know of love, if I
And sins re - lin - quish, Know of love, know of love,
And sins re - lin - quish, Know of love, I know, I know of
And sins re - lin - quish, If I know, if I know of
poco rit.
a tempo

39
mf
mp
mf
know of love, I know of love, if I know of love, if I
mf
mp
if I know, know of love, if I know, know of love,
mf
mp
love, if I know, I know of love, if I know of love, if I
mf
mp
love, I know, I know of love, know of love,
mf
mp
43
SOPRANO SOLO
mf cresc.
f
If I know, I know of love, if I know, I know of love,
S.
cresc.
f
know of love, I know of love, if I know of love, I know of love,
A.
mf cresc.
f
know of love, know of love, if I know, know of love,
T.
mf cresc.
f
know of love, I know, I know of love, if I know, I know of love,
B.
mf cresc.
f
if I know, if I know of love, I know, I know of love,
mf cresc.
f

47
mp
p
if I know of love,
if I know of love,
if I know of love,
if I know of love,
if I know of love,
Man.
52
rit.
if I know of love.
if I know of love.
if I know of love.
if I know of love.
if I know of love.
rit.
Ped.

16. Jesus Dies on the Cross

John 19: 28–30

© Oxford University Press 2013. Photocopying this copyright material is ILLEGAL.

12
filled a sponge with vi - ne - gar, and put it u - pon hys - sop, and
a little slower
14
mp
p
put it to his mouth. When Je - sus had re-ceived the vi - ne - gar, he said,
mp
p
17
JESUS
p
It is fi - nished, fi - nished.
EVANGELIST
pp dolce
And he
Ped.
Man.
20
rit.
bowed his head, and gave up the ghost.
pp dolce

17. Hymn: When I survey the Wondrous Cross

Isaac Watts (1674–1748)

'AMELIA'

© Oxford University Press 2013. Photocopying this copyright material is ILLEGAL.

11b
S.
A.
T.
B.
2.
3. See from his head, his hands, his feet,
p
blood.
3. See from his head, his hands, his feet, Sor -
p
2.
p
14
Sor - row and love flow min - gled down;
cresc.
- row and love flow min - gled down; Did
cresc.
16
Did e'er such love and sor - row meet, Or thorns com - pose so rich a
mp
e'er such love and sor - row meet, Or thorns com - pose so
mp
19
crown, or thorns com - pose so rich a crown?
mf
rich a crown, so rich a crown?
mf
mf
Ped.

Processed in England by Enigma Music Production Services, Amersham, Bucks.
Printed in England by Halstan & Co. Ltd, Amersham, Bucks.

St John Passion

BOB CHILCOTT

PARTS 1 & 2 – TACET

(1. Sing, my tongue, the glorious battle; 2. The Garden; 3. Hymn: It is a thing most wonderful; 4. Peter's Denial; 5. Meditation: Miserere, my Maker; 6. Hymn: Drop, drop, slow tears; 7. The Judgment Hall (I); 8. Hymn: Jesu, grant me this, I pray; 9. Meditation: Christ, my Beloved; 10. The Judgment Hall (II); 11. Meditation: Away vain world)

PART 3

12. Jesus is Crucified

© Oxford University Press 2013. This part may be enlarged on a photocopier to faciliate performance.

13. *Hymn: There is a green hill far away* – TACET

14. *The Crucifixion*

15. *Meditation: Jesus, my Leman* – TACET

16. *Jesus Dies on the Cross*